SIX STEPS TO A GENEROUS LIFE

SIX STEPS TO A GENEROUS LIFE

*Living Your
Commitment to Christ*

Bob Crossman

Abingdon Press

Nashville

SIX STEPS TO A GENEROUS LIFE:
LIVING YOUR COMMITMENT TO CHRIST
by Bob Crossman
Copyright © 2012 by Abingdon Press

All rights reserved.

Scripture quotations are from the Common English Bible. Copyright © 2011 by the Common English Bible. All rights reserved. Used by permission. www.CommonEnglishBible.com.

This book is printed on acid-free paper.

ISBN 978-1-4267-46901

Library of Congress Cataloging-in-Publication Data on file.

The author's personal account of the sledding experience found on page eight resembles a similar occurence noted by Norman Lucas in *Kinetic Christianity: Sermons for the Epiphany Season,* C.S.S. Publishing Company, 1979, pp. 20-26.

12 13 14 15 16 17 18 19 20 21—10 9 8 7 6 5 4 3 2
MANUFACTURED IN THE UNITED STATES OF AMERICA

Contents

Introduction: Answering the Call

All have sinned and fall short of God's glory, but all are treated as righteous freely by his grace because of a ransom that was paid by Christ Jesus.
Romans 3:23-24

"I assure you that whoever hears my word and believes in the one who sent me has eternal life and won't come under judgment but has passed from death into life."
John 5:24

My adolescent years were spent in Robbinsdale, Minnesota, just within bicycle distance from an absolutely fantastic golf course called Theodore Wirth Park. As a youth I was not impressed with Wirth Park's greens, fairways, sand traps, or water hazards. Instead, what made that golf course exciting was the terrain itself. You would not believe the hills that were on and around that golf course. To my youthful eyes, the hills were straight up and straight down. They were magnificent.

I had no interest whatsoever in golf. However, I was very interested in the golf course, especially in winter. In Minnesota, snow covered the greens and fairways from December until April. Children from my neighborhood traveled to Wirth Park carrying sleds, sheets of cardboard, trashcan lids, and almost anything they could devise to slide down the hills. There were several enticing hills on the course, but the bigger and braver children inevitably gravitated toward the tallest one, known to us as Suicide Hill.

As a young boy, Suicide Hill looked as high as Pikes Peak or Mount Everest. The long trudge to the top of that hill was agonizing, but the wild and fast ride to the bottom was worth the effort. I can remember the day some forty-five years ago when I last stood on Suicide Hill. Someone brought a marvelous piece of equipment that I had never seen before. It was wooden and flat, with a front that curled back, and a rope handle along both outer edges to hang onto. It was called a toboggan. That toboggan converted a day of routine sledding into an unforgettable experience. The person in front steered by leaning to the left or right, with six or seven of us piled on. The toboggan followed the contours of that long, long hill, plunging down at what seemed to be the speed of light.

What I remember most is the instant before the downward plunge began—the little pause at the very peak of that great hill with the valley stretching before us, when all of us clung together in anticipation of the adventure about to begin; that little fragment of time just before the first rocking motion that inched us forward over the edge. That instant is etched into my memory.

Think with me for a few minutes about that image: a toboggan poised at the crest of a hill, a toboggan that's about to begin its downward plunge but hasn't lept forward yet. Now think about your church, or your fellowship of believers, in a similar place, with that same anticipation.

The toboggan, as it sat motionless on top of the hill, possessed what is called "potential energy." It had energy yet to be actualized, energy stored that is waiting to be used. That's the way it was with the toboggan as it lay motionless at the peak of a snowy hill, waiting for us to say *yes* and give it a push.* What would it be like for you and me to say yes to God? What would it be like for us to allow God to convert our potential into reality?

What would it be like for your *church* to say yes to God? What would it be like for your church to allow God to convert *its* potential into reality?

It seems to me that such a yes to the Lord could potentially be a life-changing yes; a yes that would have implications; a yes that would cause ripples; a yes that might end up framing the rest of our earthly life; a yes that would begin a journey; a yes worth giving the rest of our lives to.

When I first began my journey with the Lord as a young adult, it involved a great deal of trust. I did not know the path my journey with the Lord might take, nor did I know the final destination. However, I did trust the Lord to guide me faithfully.

A few weeks after I began my journey, an image came to mind. I was holding a flashlight and standing on the edge of a dark forest. My flashlight only illuminated five or six feet of the path before me, yet each time I took a step I could see one more step ahead. Looking back, the image seems simplistic, but for me at the time it was powerful and reassuring—a flashlight in one hand, Jesus' hand in the other. We were on a journey together.

Another image that helped my early journey eventually became the central blueprint of this book—a set of steps. There were seasons when I boldly took a step with the Lord. And there were seasons when I said, "Lord, I'm not ready for the next step yet. I'm tired. Can we just rest on this step for a while?"

For me, there were a half-dozen steps the Lord invited me to take during those first few years (and to be honest, I'm still working on those steps). They are steps that challenged me and changed me. They are crucial steps toward a holy life, sanctification, the Cross, and becoming a deeply devoted disciple. I'll describe them in this book, in hopes that these six steps will be useful to you in your walk, ever upward, with Christ.

Prayer
Bible Reading
Church Attendance
Witness
Financial Giving
Service

My mother kept a print of Warner Sallman's famous painting, *Christ at Heart's Door,* hanging in her home. I have childhood memories of Sallman's image, in which Jesus Christ stands at a door with his hand poised ready to knock. The painting is famous in part for the absence of any outside latch on the door, indicating that we must open our hearts to Christ from within and that Christ will not force his way inside.

In many ways, my personal relationship with Christ is reflected in that image. The Lord waited patiently for me to respond and welcome his knock. In my early relationship with Christ, I opened the door of my heart. Some years later, I invited Christ to come inside rather than keeping him standing on my heart's doorstep. Years later, I welcomed him to move from the entrance hall into the living room. As my relationship with Christ matured beyond the formality of the living room, I invited him to enter the kitchen.

Do you respond to that image? Do you sense the concept of a relationship with Christ that can grow and mature, step by step on a spiritual journey together?

Are you ready to answer Christ's knock? Are you ready to open the door of your heart? Are you ready to invite him inside? Are you ready to step outward and upward with Christ?

If you were to step up your relationship with Jesus Christ, what would have to change in your heart and life?

Accepting Christ as Lord and Savior

Scott J. Jones

I was raised in The United Methodist Church, but it was more of a social experience than a true conversion and commitment to Christ.

When I left home, I quit worshiping. I didn't attend Sunday school. It wasn't that I was hostile to Christianity; I just thought organized religion wasn't worth the time. I knew that the church did good things but wasn't sure about the existence of God. Most important, I didn't have faith. I wondered what it meant to believe. I found answers through two conversations, one book, and prayer.

The first conversation came when I was hitchhiking. A truck driver picked me up and for two hours he shared his faith with me. The man's certainty about salvation was attractive. Afterward I thought, "I want what that man has."

A year later, a friend gave me a copy of C. S. Lewis's book, *The Lion, the Witch and the Wardrobe*, the first volume in *The Chronicles of Narnia* trilogy. For the first time I was exposed to powerful images that made sense of basic Christian teachings.

The second conversation was with a college friend who told me about giving her life to Christ and the peace that comes from surrendering one's heart. After that, I began praying that God would zap me with a powerful conversion experience. That experience never came. But a year later, alone in a campus ministry chapel, I was given the sense of peace my friend had described, and I came to know the love of Christ deep in my heart. I had become a disciple of Jesus.

Scott J. Jones, bishop of the Kansas Area of The United Methodist Church since 2004, served on the faculty of Perkins School of Theology, Southern Methodist University, from 1997 to 2004, where he taught the evangelism history of Christianity and Wesley studies.

1. Teach Us to Pray

"When you pray, don't be like hypocrites. They love to pray standing in the synagogues and on the street corners so that people will see them. I assure you, that's the only reward they'll get. But when you pray, go to your room, shut the door, and pray to your Father who is present in that secret place. Your Father who sees what you do in secret will reward you."
Matthew 6:5–6

My journey began with a commitment to Jesus Christ. As a young adult I accepted Christ as the Savior of my soul and the Lord of my life. I asked him to forgive my sins. I confessed that I did believe. I asked the Lord to help me live in a way that pleased him.

About three days after I made that commitment, I heard a still, small voice inside that asked, "If you really believe in me, then why don't you pray?"

Prayer was the first step for me after I made that commitment to Christ. I began to pray before I got out of bed each morning. I prayed before I ate breakfast. I prayed as I drove the car. It seemed that an hour would rarely pass without a prayer.

A frequent prayer was, "Oh, Lord, forgive me. I can't believe I just said what I said with you in the room. Help me, Lord, to control my tongue." Another frequent prayer concerned relationships at home and with friends. I was on a journey now with the Lord, and I was suddenly aware that the Lord was always by my side. This awareness constantly highlighted my sin and brought a prayer to my lips, seeking forgiveness and the strength to change.

I wasn't praying so I would be saved. I was praying because I was already saved, and I was seeking an even deeper relationship with my Savior. Prayer has helped me through times when I thought I would burst with happiness, and times when I wondered if I could go on.

* * *

I remember clearly the day my father died. He lay on his death bed in the hospital. Dad knew, Mom knew, the family knew, and the doctors knew that my father would never leave the hospital. The day finally came when Dad was unable to move, smile, or talk. However, he could see, and I could tell by the expression in his eyes that he was aware of me and understood what I was saying.

My mother stepped out of the room for a quick trip to the cafeteria. I knelt by my father's bed and held his hand. Dad and I stared into each other's eyes, and I told him my memories of so many things we had done together. I talked about camping trips, fishing trips, projects we had worked on together when I was growing up, and the way he forgave me when I totaled the family car (twice). I talked about the church building committee we both served on and about how beautiful the worship room would be when the stained glass windows were installed. I told Dad that I loved him. I recited aloud Scriptures that I had memorized, including John 3:16, Romans 8:28, Psalm 23, and John 14.

Holding Dad's hand, looking into his eyes, I prayed out loud:

> Dear Jesus, thank you for my daddy. Thank you for making him such a good father. Thank you for his love, forgiveness, and wisdom. Thank you for his baptism and for forgiving his sins. Thank you for making a home for him in heaven. Lord, as Dad lies here with one foot on earth and one foot in heaven, give him such peace inside that you are in control. Guide him on his journey from earth to heaven. Thank you, Jesus, for never leaving my daddy alone. Amen.

With tears in my eyes, I reminded my father not to be afraid. I told him that we would be okay. I told him that surely his mother and father were standing at the gates of heaven, waiting anxiously for him. I even suggested that his childhood pet, a little Boston terrier, surely must be standing by their side. I said, "I love you, Dad." My mother returned to the room, kissed him, held his hand, and said, "I love you."

Dad knew we were both there. It wasn't long before his breathing began to slow down. Ten, then seven, then five breaths a minute. Then three breaths, and then he was still.

How different the day of my father's death would

have been if I did not believe in prayer. Do you have a prayer life that gives you strength in tough times? A pastor once put it this way: "God offers us an ocean, and we choose a puddle instead."

God invites you and me to go deep. God offers to give us the depth of his presence in our lives, the depth of a life filled with joy, and the depth of power and strength in the midst of adversity. Jesus knew those depths. He lived in an ocean of constant communion with God.

Most of us choose not to go deep but to live in the shallow end of life. We choose the puddle instead of the ocean.

Now it's confession time: Some pastors say they pray two hours every day. I cannot imagine doing that. I want to tell them, "Get busy! Stop goofing off!" I confess that I don't have any slacks that are worn out at the knees from prayer.

My prayer life consists of about fifteen minutes each day. As I drive to work in the morning, I pray that God will help me use my time wisely. When I am responding to a telephone call or standing by a hospital bed, I pray that God will give me the right words to say. Before I go to sleep at night, I review in my mind the prayer cards from last Sunday's offering plate, along with the personal and private concerns I have heard, and I lift those concerns up to God. In all, it's perhaps fifteen minutes a day.

But there are times, however, when I step out of the puddle and into the ocean. Sometimes in the evening, around nine o'clock after my last appointment has ended, I walk into the darkened sanctuary. The only illumination in the room is from the cross on the altar, reflecting the golden lights from the parking lot, and the faint glow of the stained glass windows. I kneel by the altar or sit in the front row. I often find my eyes are filled with tears. Some of the tears are for my own sin and shortcomings. Some of the tears come when I read the prayer cards from Sunday morning, where members have poured out their hearts. In the midst of my tears I sense that God is crying too—that God hears these prayers for broken marriages, broken hopes, broken bodies, and broken dreams. There in the night I'm in the ocean, surrounded by the presence of God.

I have an invitation for you. Move from the puddle to the ocean. Allow God to hold you, and mold you, and empower you.

How might your prayer life move from the puddle to the ocean?

Prayer Made Easy

Olu Brown

A well-known office supply store has a popular marketing tool called the "easy button." It sends a clear message that dealing with the employees, locating items, and checking out at the register should be easy for the customer. I am glad the business world has finally discovered that in our fast-paced, ever-changing lives, people need fewer steps, less process, and simpler systems. However, I am not sure if this is the case in the spiritual world, especially when it comes to prayer.

My personal struggle is that I have had difficulty maintaining a consistent and fruitful prayer life. I now realize the barrier is within me: all my crazy, preprogrammed, learned expectations concerning prayer. I believe I have been making prayer too difficult and not "easy."

In Mark 8, Jesus fed more than five thousand people with a meal the size of an appetizer at your favorite restaurant. He lifted the appetizer to God and offered a prayer that was simple and straight to the point. No frills! He didn't go to a special place, wear fancy clothes, or recite a unique liturgy. He said what was on his mind and became the catalyst for one of the greatest miracles of all time.

For me, this example of prayer is truly a relief—no frills, just genuine prayer. My hope for you is that you don't develop a prayer life with thousands of steps or inflexible rules. Keep prayer easy, and see God's power revealed.

Olu Brown, the lead pastor of Impact Church in downtown Atlanta, Georgia, has helped make Impact one of the fastest-growing new churches in America. Impact Church is a multicultural gathering of people who are committed to sharing the love of Christ with the world and doing church differently.

2. Reading the Bible Daily

You must be doers of the word and not only hearers who mislead themselves. Those who hear but don't do the word are like those who look at their faces in a mirror. They look at themselves, walk away, and immediately forget what they were like. But there are those who study the perfect law, the law of freedom, and continue to do it. They don't listen and then forget, but they put it into practice in their lives. They will be blessed in whatever they do.
James 1:22–25

In those early weeks of my journey with the Lord, I heard another still, small voice that asked, "If you really believe in me, then why aren't you reading my book?"

I found the black Bible with red-trimmed pages that I received in the third grade. I'm sad to report that the book was in really good shape. It had hardly been read at all.

I started with the Gospel of Matthew. When I reached the Sermon on the Mount in the fifth chapter, I clearly remember thinking, "Who rewrote this thing? It's not like I remember at all." The words had come alive. It was as if it had been rewritten just for me. I was finding answers to my prayers.

I bought another copy of the Bible in paperback so I could carry it less conspicuously in my backpack. I started highlighting the "good parts" with a pink felt-tip pen. Looking back at that Bible, I find that I highlighted scattered passages through the New Testament and the entire book of James. I was on a journey, personally discovering those ancient, holy, sacred words.

I wasn't reading the Bible so that I would be saved. I was reading the Bible because I was already saved, and I was seeking an even deeper relationship with my Savior.

* * *

In the Scripture at the beginning of this chapter, James is offering a challenge for us to take God's word seriously enough that it changes our behavior. James invites us to listen to God's word, to accept the truth of what it reveals, and to change our behavior accordingly.

It's not easy to listen to God's word. How many times do you hear the Bible read from the pulpit or read it yourself, but the words don't sink in? It's hard to listen. It's hard to let the words sink in.

Back a hundred years ago, when the telegraph was the fastest method of long-distance communication, a young man applied for a job as a Morse code operator. Answering an ad in the newspaper, he went to the office to apply for the job. When he arrived, he entered a large, busy room filled with noise and clatter, including the sound of a telegraph in the background. A sign on the receptionist's desk instructed job applicants to fill out a form and wait until they were summoned to enter the inner office.

The young man filled out his form and sat down in the waiting area with seven other applicants. After a few minutes, the young man stood up and walked into the inner office. Naturally the other applicants perked up, wondering what was going on. Soon the employer escorted the young man out of the office and said to the other applicants, "Thank you for applying, but the job has just been filled."

The other applicants began grumbling, and one spoke up, saying, "Wait a minute, I don't understand. We never got a chance to be interviewed. And to top it off, this guy comes in last and you hire him. That's not fair!"

The employer said, "I'm sorry you feel that way. You all had the same opportunity. During the last several minutes while you've been sitting here, didn't you hear the telegraph key clicking? It was sending the following words in Morse code: 'If you understand this message, then come right in. The job is yours.' None of you heard it or understood it. This young man did. The job is his!"

Far too often, we let the words of the Bible drift in one ear and float out the other. The first chapter of James makes it clear: Don't do that! James writes that not only do we need to listen, but we need to accept the truth of what the Scripture reveals to us.

Tom Slinkard tells the story of a man who was driving down a road. A woman drove toward him from the opposite direction. As they passed each other, the woman leaned out her car window and yelled, "Pig!" The man, incensed, leaned out his window and yelled back at her.

They each continued on their way. As the man rounded the next curve, he crashed into a huge pig that was standing in the middle of the road. Thankfully the man was unhurt, but his car was a total wreck.

The man heard her message but did not understand or accept it. When it comes to the Bible, we not only need to hear God's word, but to understand it and accept it as valid and important for our daily lives.

There are many Christians who underline and mark the pages of the Bible. There are fewer Christians who allow the Bible to make a positive mark on their lives.

In James's letter, he says that we become motivated to change by looking into the mirror of God's word. He writes: "Those who hear but don't do the word are like those who look at their faces in a mirror. They look at themselves, walk away, and immediately forget what they were like" (James 1: 23-24).

Normally, people look in a mirror for a reason. If they see that their hair is out of place, they fix it. If they see a piece of lettuce between their teeth, they remove it. If they see that they cut themselves shaving, they stop the bleeding.

When you look into the Bible and see something in your own life that may need to be fixed, don't turn away. Take it as an opportunity, a gift if you will, to ask God for the courage, guidance, and the strength to change.

How could the Bible become the source of your strength, your guide, and your measuring stick for truth?

God's Measuring Stick

James W. Moore

Some years ago, there was a great professor at Centenary College, Dean R. E. Smith, a very distinctive looking man who wore a black patch over one eye. Dean Smith was a saintly man, a brilliant scholar, an outstanding communicator, a true friend to his students, and a legend in his own time.

In one of his most famous lectures, Dean Smith spoke to his students about how we discover truth and how we determine what is genuine and authentic. After some discussion, Dean Smith suddenly asked, "How wide is my desk?" The students would look at the desk and then make their best guesses. A variety of answers would ring out.

"I think it's about 72 inches wide."

"No, I believe it's more like 68 inches wide."

"Looks like 75 to me."

"I'm going to guess 74 inches."

Then some wise guy from the back of the room would say, "71 and 5/16?" and everyone would laugh.

Then Dean Smith would say, "Those are all pretty good guesses, but one of them is more nearly true than the others. Now, how do we determine which one is most accurate? How do we decide which answer is most nearly right?"

There would be complete silence for a moment in the classroom, and then someone would ask tentatively, "Get a measuring stick?"

"That's right," Dean Smith would say. "To determine which one is closest to the truth, we have to get a measuring stick and measure it!"

Then he would go to the blackboard. He would take a piece of chalk, and, in silence, draw the outline of a cross. With the chalk, he would trace over and over the outline of the cross, letting it dramatically sink into the hearts and minds of those students.

Then he would stand back, point to that cross, and say, "There's your measuring stick! There's your measuring stick for truth!"

With the Bible comes God's encouraging promise: Here's your compass. Here's your guiding light. Here's your measuring stick for truth.

Study the Bible. Memorize its key verses. Get the Scriptures inside of you. Write them on your heart. Immerse yourselves in the Bible. Learn the key themes of the Bible. And the Bible will be your measuring stick to show you what is true and right and good.

James W. Moore, popular speaker and preacher, has written more than forty books including Yes, Lord, I Have Sinned, But I Have Several Excellent Excuses; God Was Here, and I Was Out to Lunch; When Grief Breaks Your Heart; *and* There's a Hole in Your Soul That Only God Can Fill. *He and his wife, June, live in Fairview, Texas.*

*Reprinted from James W. Moore, *Standing on the Promises or Sitting on the Premises?* Nashville: Abingdon Press, 1995, pp. 113–15.

3. Let Us Go to the House of the Lord

Just like a deer that craves streams of water,
my whole being craves you, God.
My whole being thirsts for God,
for the living God.
When will I come and see God's face?
Psalm 42:1–2

Suddenly I was not going to worship to please my mother or in obedience to my father. I was going because I wanted to. I was on a journey with the Lord. In worship I was discovering the context of my new-found relationship with the Lord. Through the music I was finding expression for my praise, thanksgiving, and hope, and the sermons were inspiring. I clearly remember thinking, "Brother Ramsey is sure a better preacher than he used to be."

Looking back, I now know that I had become a better listener. The sermons were about me, my struggles, my sin, and my future.

I wasn't in worship seeking salvation. I was in worship because I was already saved, and I was seeking an even deeper relationship with my Savior.

* * *

On Sunday afternoons, if I happen to encounter a sales clerk, I frequently ask, "Do you have to work every Sunday morning, or do you occasionally get to attend worship?" That simple question almost always elicits a friendly conversation and gives me the opportunity to invite them to attend Sunday evening worship.

My mother was passionate about inviting people to worship. She was the office manager for a poultry supply company, which meant that all customers had to come to her office to place their orders. After worship on Sundays she would pick up a dozen or so leftover worship bulletins and take them to work with her. Then on Mondays she would simply ask each customer, "How was church yesterday?" If customers hesitated or gave some excuse, she would quickly hand them a worship bulletin with the words, "My husband and I really enjoy First Church. Why don't you sit with us next Sunday?" If the customer was an active church attender, her simple question introduced a friendly conversation and often began a new Christian friendship.

I have frequently followed my Mother's example on Mondays. I can report dozens of households who became active participants of my church as a result.

As you consider inviting others to worship, I encourage you to step up your own worship attendance. In worship we find our center and our focus for life. Kara Newell puts it this way: "My mother is a potter and I've spent many happy hours watching her prepare the wet clay, plop a soggy lump of it on the wheel, start the wheel, and slowly draw the clay up into whatever form she has chosen. But, I've also watched her stop and start the process over and over when she's been unable to center the clay properly. She knows that whatever comes from uncentered clay will not be usable."

That's true for us too, isn't it? Unless we become clay in the Potter's hands and allow ourselves to be centered in God, we will not be useful in the ways that we are called to minister. In worship, we learn how to center our lives on God. And being so well-centered every Sunday, we are able to fully live the other six days.

My friends, in worship Jesus does indeed come. In worship we place ourselves where miraculous things can happen: our sins can be forgiven, our hearts can be purified, our minds can glimpse the mind of Christ, our hands can be empowered to serve the Lord, and our lives can move closer to the patterns that Christ exemplified.

In worship we hear the invitation to move one step closer to becoming a deeply devoted disciple of Jesus Christ.

Do you attend worship, ready to be "clay" in the Potter's hands?

Faithful Worship Attendance

Rick Bezet

At New Life Church, just after we built our first building in Conway, Arkansas, a very distinguished-looking man approached me after the service with red eyes, evidently from crying. Standing behind him were his wife and two children. With quivering lips, the man told me that this was his family's first visit to our church and that he loved it, but that he had a serious question: "Can this church accept a man like me, who shoved his wife into the wall last week while his kids were watching? Can the church allow a person who struggles with anger to come?" His wife's eyes were silently saying, "Please say yes." It took a lot of courage for this man to approach me.

I told him that God is able to heal his anger as though it were never there and even to establish him as a leader who can help other families. This has actually become true, and this family serves faithfully in our small group ministry and in welcoming people into our foyer during weekend services.

This man made an adjustment that some people never make. That first day he came in need; he was a "consumer." He needed something we could offer to him, an encounter with a real Savior. He could have kept coming back to church, always looking for another way Jesus could meet his needs, but instead he became a "contributor" and gave to others.

Rick Bezet is the founder and lead pastor of New Life Church in Central Arkansas. NLC was America's fastest growing church in 2009, according to Outreach Magazine. *Rick is also a founding board member and overseer of the Association of Related Churches, a nationwide church-planting organization.*

4. You Shall Be My Witnesses

"You will receive power when the Holy Spirit has come upon you, and you will be my witnesses in Jerusalem, in all Judea and Samaria, and to the end of the earth."
Acts 1:8

It was awkward at first, introducing faith into my relationships. Up to that point, my relationships had been built around other issues. Now I felt compelled to discover ways to introduce new conversations. It was easier than I thought it would be. My circle of friends at work had thoughts and concerns about their own faith, and they welcomed occasional conversations about religion. To my great surprise, within six months I was meeting with twenty of my friends every Friday evening to share, pray, and even sing songs of faith.

When you take the step of witnessing, I wonder what reaction you will experience. There's no way to know for sure. However, I do know that the Lord will hold your hand and safely guide you to discover words to share your faith in a compelling way.

* * *

A friend of mine wears a class ring on his right hand. When he bought that ring in college many years ago, he was given an opportunity to choose the shape displayed on the face of the ring. He chose a small cross.

Years later my friend was on a plane flight, and a woman sat next to him. After they had been in the air for a while, she happened to notice his ring. "Are you some kind of religious person?" she asked. "That cross on your ring must mean you're a Christian or something."

He told her that indeed he was a Christian. She smiled and said, "You know, I used to go to church myself when I was a little girl. But I haven't gone for years. I don't know why. I just haven't."

She went on to say, "Life's been pretty tough for me. I got pregnant when I was fifteen and married when I was sixteen, to a guy who was nine years older than me. We divorced a year later, and I got married again when I was nineteen. I've been married and divorced four times now, to men who beat me and took advantage of me. I don't think marriage is for me."

My friend said, "I'm sorry. I'm so sorry to hear that. What a disappointment that must be for you."

And she continued, "Yeah, it really is. I mean, I think marriage ought to be for life, a sacred thing, you know? That's what the Bible says, doesn't it? But it hasn't been that way for me."

My friend just listened as she continued her story. Then she said something that gave him an opportunity to share his faith in Jesus Christ. She asked, "Do you think going to church could help me?"

And my friend said, "Of course. But even more than that, Jesus Christ can help you. Christ can help you start putting your life back together. You know, the Lord knows who you are, and the Lord is inside of you right now."

Hearing those words, the woman began to cry. "I can't imagine that," she said. " I really can't. Christ is inside of me?"

My friend smiled and said, "Yes, he is. And he is not judging you either. He's there to help you. He's the best friend you'll ever have."

Believe it or not, the two of them prayed together as they sat on that plane. My friend asked the Lord to come into her heart, to make a difference in her life, to help her find a new life and a new beginning for herself. And you know what? As they were walking off the plane, she turned around and said, "There's a church not far from my house, and I think I'll go there next Sunday."

And she did. How do I know? It just so happened that at 10:45 the next Sunday, as my friend was going into worship at his own church, he saw her walk into the lobby.

The point is this: We don't have to force ourselves on strangers. God is always opening doors for us to be witnesses. Maybe it will happen tomorrow morning in the carpool, maybe on the Internet tonight, maybe sitting next to a stranger on your next flight, maybe with a member of your own family tomorrow. But make no mistake about it: God will open doors for you to be a witness.

Will you realize when God opens that door?
Will you speak for God when it happens?

An Invitation

Bob Pierson

The experience of coming to know Christ can often be through a simple invitation. In John 1:40-46 we have two stories: Andrew inviting Peter to meet Jesus, and then Philip inviting Nathaniel. These stories sometimes seem so basic, but frequently the faith is transmitted in this simple way.

Doug was going through a difficult time. He and his wife were divorced, and the children were teenagers. There was a lot of chaos in his life. He was not a committed Christian, nor was he involved in the church. He was searching.

Doug's fifteen-year-old son Adam was invited by one of his friends to a concert at a church. Adam visited the church, met other teenagers, and eventually stayed. Over time he became deeply committed to Christ. Next Adam invited his twelve-year-old sister, and she was touched by the invitation. She went and became involved in the youth group. Soon after she made a commitment to Christ. The two children then invited their mother. In the midst of her struggle with divorce, she too committed her life to Christ and became involved in the church.

Doug, still distant from God, was the next target of their efforts. One night they invited Doug to a concert in which Adam was involved. Doug was touched by the experience, started attending the church, and later became involved himself. Out of that experience,

Doug grew deeply in the Christian faith, matured in leadership, and became chairman of the evangelism committee. The excitement of following Christ came in stages for Doug. He is now deeply committed to Christ and leading the church in evangelism. He has just written a new book entitled *Reach*, which describes how social media can help the church reach more people for Christ.

Bob Pierson is founder and Executive Director of Leadership Nexus. He served as Senior Pastor of Christ Church in Tulsa, Oklahoma, for 37 years, increasing attendance from 200 to over 1600. Leadership Nexus exists to help the church be more effective in proclaiming the Gospel to the world.

5. Financial Giving

Remember the Lord Jesus' words: "It is more blessed to give than to receive."
Acts 20:35

Everyone should give whatever they have decided in their heart. They shouldn't give with hesitation or because of pressure. God loves a cheerful giver.
2 Corinthians 9:7

To be honest, it never bothered me to pass an empty offering plate down the pew. I saw that other people were giving money, but I felt no inclination to do so myself.

In the early months of my new journey with the Lord, I remember asking my girlfriend to attend a Christian concert. Near the end of the concert, the musicians invited everyone to open their wallets and give money for a particular mission project. I believe it was the first time it dawned on me that there are a great number of missions and religious institutions that simply cannot function without the gift of financial resources. It later occurred me that I needed to give, not because the church needed my money but because I needed to give to establish Godly priorities my life. I needed to give because the Lord had already given so much for me.

When you take the step of financial giving, I wonder how long it will take you to reach the Biblical minimum of a ten percent tithe? I wonder if you will discover the joy of giving? I wonder if giving will become a priority in your life? I wonder.

* * *

When Christian theologian and Methodism founder John Wesley was a college student at Oxford, a custodian knocked on his door one cold night as he was studying. John answered and they talked briefly. As the custodian was leaving, John noticed that the man had on a thin jacket. John remarked, "You ought to put on a heavier coat." The custodian responded, "This is the only coat I have, and I thank God for this coat."

When Wesley realized the man did not have enough money to buy warm clothes, he asked if he had enough to buy food. The custodian's reply was essentially the same: "I have had nothing today but water to drink, but I thank God for the water."

Wesley was getting uncomfortable with the conversation and said something about it being time for the man to get home and crawl into a warm bed. And the custodian responded, "I thank God I have a dry floor to sleep on tonight."

John, deeply moved by the man's simple faith in God, asked, "You thank God when you have nothing to wear, nothing to eat, and no warm bed upon which to lie. What else do you thank God for?"

The custodian replied, "I thank God that he has given me the gift of life, a heart to love him, and a deep desire to serve him. What more could a man ever want?"

John Wesley was so moved by the custodian's words that he wrote in his journal that night, "I shall never forget that man. He convinced me that there's something in religion to which I am a stranger."

The encounter led John Wesley to develop a strong opinion about money. Later he wrote: "Make all you can. Save all you can. Give all you can." And he did just that. Wesley gave everything away. Upon his death, there was hardly any estate at all. He had lived very modestly, so he could give everything to the building of new churches, to the purchase of religious books for classes to use, and to support ministry to widows, orphans, and prisoners.

If you were to live by the slogan
"Make all you can, save all you can, give all you
can," how would your lifestyle change?

You Tithe But . . .

J. Clif Christopher

The other day I was visiting with a young man who told me about his father, who lived in a city not too far away. He said that his dad faithfully sent a check for child support and would buy birthday and Christmas presents, but rarely expressed a desire to be with him. As the young man spoke, I could see the pain in his eyes and on his face. He said that even in the summer when he went to see his father, the father was often busy and would send him off to a cousin or family friend. It was great to get the money and gifts, but more than anything the young man wanted love. He wanted a relationship that his father obviously could not or would not provide.

Not long after that, I found myself talking with a woman who was angry with her ex-husband for talking on the phone with their child and coming to be with him, but who would not pay child support or purchase school supplies. The woman said, "He thinks withholding the money is just hurting me and not his son, but it is hurting his son. I cannot buy my son all the things he needs to wear to school and dress properly. The attention is nice, but it is hollow without money to back it up."

All of this got me to thinking about how I feel about tithing. I have been a long-time tither, giving God at least ten percent of my earnings, and on occasion I have lapsed into thinking that now that I have tithed, I can do exactly as I please. On the other hand, some may want to "trade" tithing for giving their time, assuming that God has some sort of point system, and they can gain enough points in one area to make up for another.

I found myself remembering Matthew 23:23, where Jesus said (to paraphrase), "You tithe but....." Jesus was not saying that giving the tithe was bad, not at all. He was saying that only giving the tithe and not loving God or loving our neighbor misses the point. In other words, it's not our money that Jesus is after, but a relationship. God wants us to be in a loving relationship with him more than anything else, and tithing is and should be one part of that expression of love. I should want to tithe, not so I will get something in return. I should want to at least tithe because of the simple fact that I love God and I'm so grateful for all he has done for me.

A father who says he wants to have a relationship with a child but refuses to share a portion of his wealth with him is not a father who truly loves his child. And a father who only sends his child money, no matter how much, but does not desire to spend time with him, is not a father who truly loves his child. Both cases reveal a person who is too much in love with himself, a person who values money or guarding personal time more than a loving relationship.

Tithing is important to me, but not to gain points or go to heaven; it is important in order to have and sustain the kind of loving relationship with my heavenly Father that is necessary for me to live.

J. Clif Christopher founded the Horizons Stewardship Company in 1992 following twenty years in pastoral ministry. He has led consultations in over 400 churches, conferences, synods, and dioceses in all phases of building, finance, and church growth. He is the author of Not Your Parents' Offering Plate *and* Whose Offering Plate Is It?

6. Hands-on Service in Jesus' Name

There are different spiritual gifts but the same Spirit; and there are different ministries and the same Lord; and there are different activities but the same God who produces all of them in everyone. A demonstration of the Spirit is given to each person for the common good.
1 Corinthians 12:1, 4–7

One summer I noticed weeds growing in the flowerbed around the sign in front of my church. Each week the weeds spread and grew taller. As the weeks passed, I became increasingly angry that no one was maintaining that flowerbed around the sign and that it was giving a poor impression to folks who drove by. One Sunday in worship, I mentioned in prayer what I had noticed. In response, I heard a small voice saying, "I have already called someone to maintain the church flower beds, but he isn't getting the job done. He thinks it's someone else's job." I almost laughed out loud as I prayed, "I hear you, Lord. I will maintain your flower beds." That very week on my day off, I was on my knees praying, spraying, and pulling. The next week, others joined me in getting blisters for Jesus. In a few weeks, formal teams were at work with edgers, mowers, and leaf blowers. We were all discovering the joy of serving in Jesus' name.

I went on to discover ways to serve the Lord

through the United Way, Boys & Girls Club, mission trips, and church camps.

When you take the step of serving in Jesus' name, I wonder where you will serve? I wonder where you will "get blisters" in Jesus' name? I don't know the answer. What I do know is that the Lord will take this journey of service with you and will guide you to wonderful places where you can make a difference by the sweat of your brow and the strength of your hands.

Maybe you'll be like Mrs. Harrison. She was about sixty years old. Although her own children had grown up, married, and moved out of state, God had given her a special love for teenagers. So, Mrs. Harrison was at church every Sunday night. She made sure the youth group ran smoothly. She coordinated parents to bring snack suppers. She had a Wednesday morning prayer breakfast for the youth before school. On those mornings, she brought doughnuts, orange juice, and milk, and she opened the sanctuary for the youth to kneel in prayer before breakfast. She did this for years and years without fail. She was like a second grandmother to the youth.

Has it ever dawned on you that *you* could be a Mrs. Harrison at your church?

Let me tell you about Mr. Edwards. He worked for the phone company. He was on the road a great deal, but that didn't keep him from serving the Lord at church. Mr. Edwards was a parent with two sons in the youth group. He not only loved his boys but he had enough patience and love for all the youth in the church, including me. Every Sunday night he would pick out three or four of us to do the program for the next Sunday. He met with us midweek and helped us put the Sunday evening program together, including skits, Scripture reading, or maybe a video clip to watch. He also taught the youth Sunday school class. He was like a second father to our youth group. Has it ever dawned on you that *you* could be a Mr. Edwards at your church?

Let me tell you about Mr. Keller. He was president of the bank downtown and had a big house in a new subdivision. He also had a special place in his heart for the youth at church, and those of us in the youth group knew it. Whether it was a Friday night discussion group or a Monday evening prayer meeting, his home was always available. At work, his office door was always open to us. Every time I walked into the bank, he would walk over to me at the teller counter and speak with me. I had less than twenty dollars in the bank, but he wanted to invest his time in my life. Did any of the youth need a summer job? He would help. Did we have problems at home? He would listen. Did anyone need an adult to talk to? His door was open. Has it ever dawned on you that *you* could be a Mr. Keller at your church?

Then there's Marcia. She was a college student— too old for the youth group. But she gave her time to the youth ministry all summer. Youth trip? She would be a driver. Youth swim party? She was in the pool. Prayer vigil? She brought Cokes. She was like a big sister to the youth. Has it ever dawned on you that *you* could be a Marcia at your church?

Of course, there are other ministries at church besides youth. Let me tell you about Fran. She was in her mid-seventies and had more than her share of health problems. However, she was at church every Sunday, standing by the door before worship and shaking every hand, saying, "I'm so glad you are here today." Fran was at the door after worship, too. "Thank you for coming today," she would say. "I hope to see you next Sunday." On Mondays, she sent handwritten notes to worship guests the first seven times they visited. On Tuesdays she sent handwritten notes to any members who had missed three or more Sundays. On Wednesdays, as a volunteer at the local hospital, she would stop by to visit any patients related to the church.Has it ever dawned on you that *you* could be a Fran at your church?

What do you want to be? What do you want do? You can do it in Christ's name by serving.

What do you want to do with your life?
What imprint do you want to leave on this earth?

A Man Named Ernie

Minerva G. Carcaño

Early one Saturday morning I found myself on my knees in the dirt, next to a row of young people. Together we were planting flowers around the small, simple home of a man whom these young people helped to emerge from poverty. They had met the man at a homeless shelter, given him a sandwich, and prayed for him. When they left him behind at that homeless shelter, it had disturbed their spirits.

"How can we just walk away and leave this man homeless?" they asked themselves.

Ernie was his name. His struggle and his spirit so moved these young people that they couldn't forget him. They started taking Ernie to church with them on Sundays. They convinced their parents to help them lift Ernie out of his poverty. Ernie, however, didn't want to be patronized; he'd had enough of that in his life. The young people knew they didn't want to do anything that would hurt Ernie. Thus began a shared journey of learning what it means to serve others in the name of Christ. In fact, the journey transformed their lives. Hearing their story, I was moved to join them.

On bended knee, I learned that the young people and their parents had helped Ernie by listening to his needs and hopes then surrounding him with the kind of help Ernie felt he needed. In return, Ernie pledged to live responsibly, abstaining from alcohol and drugs, showing up for appointments, and being truthful and honest in all matters. Ernie needed a doctor, so they found one who would see him as a gift of mercy. He needed a job, so one of the parents helped him prepare a resume, apply for a job, practice for his job interview, and accompany him to the interview. When Ernie got the job, he needed a car but didn't want a handout, so they found a family who had a car they were willing to sell and who were willing to wait until Ernie received his first paycheck to begin to pay for the car. The same was true of a house. It was important to Ernie to own a home he had worked for himself. The youth and their parents, along with other church members who had joined them by this time, made it possible for Ernie to receive a loan so he would have the money to buy his dream home—a small mobile home in a stable, safe, and secure community. It was at that mobile home, Ernie's home, where I found myself on that Saturday.

These young people and Ernie treated each other like family. Ernie told us what he wanted planted and where. The young people went in and out of Ernie's home with the ease of those who know they are welcomed. Though they came from families of economic means and Ernie had just come out of poverty, I did not once notice the kind of alienation that so often rears its ugly head when there are social and economic differences between persons—quite the contrary. Watching and listening, I realized that Ernie and these young people had, in the spirit of the historic Eucharistic prayer, become one. For generations, Christian disciples have prayed that they might become one with Christ, one with each other, and one in ministry to all the world. That prayer had been fulfilled in this wondrous community of faith between young people and a once-homeless man. The love among them was deep and authentic, as together they dreamed of ways to help others.

When I asked how it all happened, Ernie told me that the young people gave him a new life by loving him with the very love of Christ Jesus. The young people disagreed, saying it had been Ernie who showed *them* the love of Christ. He taught them about life and the sustaining grace of God. His profound gratitude deepened their commitment to being servant leaders in the world.

I could see that both answers were right. The generous sharing of Christ's love had transformed them all. And by the end of that day, I had been transformed as well.

Minerva G. Carcaño is the first Hispanic woman to be elected to the episcopacy of The United Methodist Church. She is Bishop of the Phoenix Episcopal Area and serves as the official spokesperson for The United Methodist Council of Bishops on the issue of immigration.

If you liked this book,
you'll love the church program.

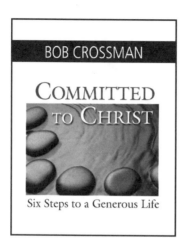

BOB CROSSMAN

COMMITTED
TO CHRIST

Six Steps to a Generous Life

This six-week stewardship campaign includes a kickoff Sunday and six weeks of sermons, worship, study, and devotions around the six commitments of Christian discipleship: prayer, Bible reading, worship, service, financial giving, and witness.

Abingdon Press / May 2012

Get more information at:
AbingdonPress.com

About the Author

Bob Crossman has over 35 years of experience as a pastor and has served as pastor or staff member in congregations from 13 to 3000 members. As Director of the New Church Leadership Institute for the Arkansas Conference of the United Methodist Church and a Ministry Strategist with Horizons Stewardship, he conducts workshops across the country on topics of wholistic stewardship, developing a vision, and overcoming growth barriers in a range of settings, from new church starts to established congregations. Bob has been the recipient of the Denman Evangelism Award and received a doctorate from SMU in evangelism.